I0402231

COMPOUND INTEREST SECRETS

"GROW YOUR WEALTH JUST LIKE THE BIG GUYS"

Justin Harrison

Compound interest is the 8th wonder of the world. He who understands it earns it... he who does not pays it!

~ Albert Einstein

~ FOREWORD ~

Compound interest is probably the most neglected topic ever to be taught in schools.

If it works for you, you will create a fortune, however, if it works against you, it will be like swimming against an ocean current trying to make it out on the other side.

This book contains the vital piece of information that is missing from our education system today, the information that is absolutely essential in terms of personal finance.

In Compound Interest Secrets Justin simplifies the subject and by making use of metaphors and real-life examples, he paints a clear picture where you will see compound interest in action and how you can use it to your advantage.

If you follow the advice Justin gives in this book, you will never want to make any credit card debt again and you will become obsessed with finding investment opportunities where you can make compound interest work for you.

If you follow Justin's advice in this book, you will flourish financially and if you have children, teach this infor-

mation to them because it will shape their future for the better.

David Bester

TABLE OF CONTENTS

~ FOREWORD ~

TABLE OF CONTENTS

INTRODUCTION

COMPOUNDING POWER EXPLAINED

COMPOUND INTEREST VS NORMAL INTEREST

COMPOUND INTEREST ON DEBT

COMPOUND INTEREST AND INVESTING

LEVERAGING COMPOUND INTEREST

PATIENCE & DISCIPLINE

MOTIVATION FROM PROFESSIONAL INVESTORS

BUILDING A FAMILY DYNASTY

BEST PLACES TO INVEST LONG TERM

CLOSING THOUGHTS

~ ACKNOWLEDGEMENTS ~

INTRODUCTION

C ompound interest expands money, infinitely. It grows investments exponentially. It harnesses the power of time itself. No get rich quick idea or secret formula can produce the same result as compound interest over time.

Consider the ancient Chinese tale of the chessboard and the grain of rice. The Emperor of China loved the game of chess so much that he rewarded the inventor of the game with one wish to reward him...

The inventor seized the opportunity and "invented" compound interest on the spot. He replied that he wanted one grain of rice on the first square of the chessboard, two grains on the second square, four on the third and so on through the 64th square.

Little did the Emperor realize the power of this seemingly modest request. But by the time he would reach the last square, he would need 18 million trillion grains of rice. This would be more than enough to cover the entire surface of the earth.

The clever inventor did not gain all the rice in China, instead, he lost his head. But he did give us the power of compounding in the process.

And as you are about to discover, such is the power of

the compounding effect.

COMPOUNDING POWER EXPLAINED

Assume you start out on January 1 by saving 1 cent, and that you double the amount saved every day (i.e 2 cents on January 2, 4 cents on January 3 and so on).

How long do you think it will take to save $1 million? Would you assume it would take 100 years, 10 years, a 1 year?

DAY 1	$0.01	DAY 15	$163.84
DAY 2	$0.02	DAY 16	$327.68
DAY 3	$0.04	DAY 17	$655.36
DAY 4	$0.08	DAY 18	$1,310.72
DAY 5	$0.16	DAY 19	$2,621.44
DAY 6	$0.32	DAY 20	$5,242.88
DAY 7	$0.64	DAY 21	$10,485.76
DAY 8	$1.28	DAY 22	$20,971.52
DAY 9	$2.56	DAY 23	$41,943.04
DAY 10	$5.12	DAY 24	$83,886.08
DAY 11	$10.24	DAY 25	$167,772.16
DAY 12	$20.48	DAY 26	$335,544.32
DAY 13	$40.96	DAY 27	$671,088.64
DAY 14	$81.92	DAY 28	$1,342,177.28

~ Compounding Affect Illustrated ~

The answer is just 28 days! In fact, in 28 days you will have saved $1,342,177.28

Realistically, investments that increase by a 100% on a daily basis don't exist. However, even with much lower returns, you'll still want compound interest working for you.

But that's not the end of the story when it comes to compound interest.

What I'm going to explain next within this course is something that no one ever taught you. By the end of this course, you will understand the most important principle of wealth creation missed by 99% of people. If applied, it will unlock a whole new world for you.

Let's dive right in!

COMPOUND INTEREST VS NORMAL INTEREST

S imply put, compounding interest refers to the fact that the interest you receive will be calculated not only on the principal amount that you invested but also on prior interest amounts added to your investment.

That is, the interest you earn will also add interest upon interest and will keep doing this as long as you keep reinvesting your interest earned.

An example of simple interest:

Simple interest is what you earn on your initial investment, known as the "principal amount". For example, if you earn 10% on $10,000, you will have $11,000 after year 1. The additional $1,000 earned is what's known as simple interest.

However, if you reinvest the interest from year 1 along with the principal amount, in year 2 you will start earning interest not only on the principal amount but also on the simple interest earned in year 1.

So at the same interest rate of 10%, you will have $12,100 ($11,000 +10%) at the end of year 2, meaning that you earned an additional $100 in compound interest (see table below) because you now earned interest on your interest.

YEAR	PRINCIPAL AMOUNT	INTEREST EARNED	TOTAL	COMPOUND INTEREST EARNED
1	$10,000.00	$1,000.00	$11,000.00	
2	$11,000.00	$1,100.00	$12,100.00	$100.00
3	$12,100.00	$1,210.00	$13,310.00	$110.00
4	$13,310.00	$1,331.00	$14,641.00	$121.00
5	$14,641.00	$1,464.10	$16,105.10	$133.10

~ Interest Illustrated At 10% ~

When you start to understand that you can earn interest on your interest, it's basically understanding that this is the closest thing to free money you will ever find.

Think about it for a second. After your initial investment you get paid interest on that investment, thereafter (provided you don't withdraw the money) you start earning interest on the interest you have been paid.

THAT'S FREE MONEY RIGHT THERE!

COMPOUND INTEREST ON DEBT

Now if you feeling slightly overjoyed at the idea of compound interest, let me stop you dead in your tracks and explain the other side of the "coin".

Compound interest on debt is the very reason the debt trap exists. Essentially you are not only repaying the principal amount borrowed but often you are repaying interest on interest (compound interest).

When you use credit and don't pay off the entire amount by the initial due date, for example, you are setting yourself up to pay compound interest.

Here's a very simple example showing how it works:

PAYBACK PERIOD	PRINCIPAL DEBT	INTEREST CHARGED	BALANCE DUE
Month 1	$500.00	$500 * 15% / 12	$506.25
Month 2	$506.25	$506.25 * 15% / 12	$512.58
Month 3	$512.58	$512.58 * 15% / 12	$518.99

You can see how adding the interest back to the balance and then charging interest on that new balance can add up quickly.

Of course, this example is oversimplified. No repayments are made in this example, so the balance continues to rise.

In the real world, you would make repayments so the balance would decrease, however, if you are not paying off the full balance, you will indeed be getting charged some compound interest and your debt would, therefore, be compounding over the long term.

Here are examples of instances where compound interest on debt becomes a trap that most people don't even see coming:

- Not making the full monthly repayments on debt,
- Making late payments,
- Increases in bank fees,
- Increases in interest rates added to the principal loan.

All of the instances above result in compound interest being charged on the debt. In most cases this can be avoided, making sure you keep more of your hard-earned money.

How to avoid compound interest on debt:

- Always make your debt repayments on schedule or ahead of time.

- Where possible try and pay more than the minimum repayment.

- Where possible try and fix your interest rates for the term of your loan.

- Where possible try and fix the fees for the term of your loan.

COMPOUND INTEREST AND INVESTING

Compound interest is one of the fundamental components in the laws of money. If people were taught about compound interest at school as part of money management, I highly doubt they would spend money the way they do, and I am absolutely certain their attitude to saving and investing would be entirely different too.

Now since we have already established that its unrealistic to double your money every day, harnessing the power of compounding will double your money over time.

To answer the question of how long it will take to double your money, we must turn to a mathematical rule on compounding called the "Rule of 72" which is used to determine how long it will take to double your money.

The Rule of 72

The Rule states that compound interest will approximately double your money within a calculable time period: that period is determined by dividing the interest rate you receive into 72. The result will be the period, in years, that it will take to double your money.

Here are two examples:

> If you earn an 8% interest on your principal investment. It will take 9 years to double your money through compound interest. This is calculated as follows: **72 Divided by 8 (the interest rate) = 9 Years**

> If you earn a 10% interest on your principal investment. It will take 7.2 years to double your money through compound interest. This is calculated as follows: **72 Divided by 10 (the interest rate) = 7.2 Years**

The power of compound interest has never been more relevant with regards to managing your personal finances, both in terms of your debt and savings.

Nothing beats simplicity.

And absolutely nothing beats doing nothing! And believe it or not, that is exactly what compound interest is all about.

Compound interest is about finding a secure investment and letting the future take its course. This is the biggest wealth secret you will ever learn. It's all about letting your investments compound and do the hard work for you.

To further illustrate the importance and power of compound interest consider that $100 invested at mere 10% annual return and left for 85 years, would be worth a whopping $329,796.90 at the end of 85 years for doing absolutely nothing.

The compounding effect is further highlighted when you look at the three examples below showing the investment value from a single investment of $100 over 3 time periods (50, years, 80 years and 85 years). The important thing to note in this illustration is that the more money you have, the faster it grows.

PRINCIPAL AMOUNT	YEARS INVESTED	INVESTMENT VALUE	COMPOUND INTEREST EARNED
$100.00	50	$11,739.09	$11,639.09
$100.00	80	$204,840.02	$204,740.02
$100.00	85	$329,896.90	$329,796.90

And finally, if you consider that all this required only a single act in the beginning, much like planting a seed, it is unfathomable why people are not planting more financial seeds.

LEVERAGING COMPOUND INTEREST

N ow that you have seen the power of compound interest and the effect it can have on the act of a single amount invested, what would happen if you were able to leverage it?

Imagine adding further fuel to your investment by:

- Increasing the rate of return (interest rate), or
- Contributing additional capital to the principal amount regularly.

What do you think the compounding effect would be if you added this kind of additional leverage? Well, the answer is it's a bit like adding rocket fuel to a supercar.

Example 1: 10% on a single principal amount invested over 50 year

If you invested $1000 initially at a 10% annual return at the end of 50 years your investment would be worth a **$117,390.85**

Example 2: 12% on a single principal amount invested over 50 year

If you invested $1000 initially at a 12% annual return at the end of 50 years your investment would be worth a **$289,002.19**

Example 3: 10% on a single principal amount invested over 50 years and an additional $1,000 added to the investment annually.

If you invested $1000 initially at a 10% annual return and added an additional $1000 a year for 49 years thereafter to the principal investment, at the end of 50 years your investment would be worth a staggering **$1,397,690.23 (That's nearly 1.4 million dollars)**

Example 4: 12% on a single principal amount invested over 50 years and an additional $1,000 added to the investment annually.

If you invested $1000 initially at a 12% annual return and added an additional $1000 a year for 49 years thereafter to the principal investment, at the end of 50 years your investment would be worth a staggering **$2,977,022.63 (That's nearly 3 million dollars)**

Now have a look at these numbers side by side to see how staggering a little bit of leverage can be over the long term:

PRINCIPAL INVESTMENT	ADDITIONAL ANNUAL INVESTMENT	RATE OF RETURN	VALUE AT THE END OF 50 YEARS
$1,000.00	$0.00	10%	$117,390.85
$1,000.00	$0.00	12%	$289,002.19
$1,000.00	$1,000.00	10%	$1,397,690.23
$1,000.00	$1,000.00	12%	**$2,977,022.63**

And if this is not already eye-opening enough, you're about to discover one of the lesser-known secrets to fully leveraging compound interest that will completely blow your mind.

Compound Interest Interval

Did you know that having the interest on your investment paid back into the investment more regularly can dramatically increase the overall value of the investment over the long term, even at the exact same interest rate?

Banks and investment houses have been taking advantage of investors for years by only paying the interest into the investments annually, and therefore decreasing the amount of compound interest they need to pay out on investments.

In many instances, investors are given the option to have their interest credited annually, quarterly or monthly. Many make the mistake of choosing the longer payout periods thinking this is a good way to force themselves to "save" the interest earned.

So using the exact same calculations from the previous example, let's take a look at the impact of receiving interest payments monthly vs annually.

PRINCIPAL INVESTMENT	ADDITIONAL ANNUAL INVESTMENT	RATE OF RETURN	VALUE AT THE END OF 50 YEARS - INTEREST CREDITED ANNUALLY	VALUE AT THE END OF 50 YEARS - INTEREST CREDITED MONTHLY	DIFFERENCE IN REURIN
$1,000.00	$0.00	10%	$117,390.85	$145,369.92	$27,979.07
$1,000.00	$0.00	12%	$289,002.19	$391,583.40	$102,581.21
$1,000.00	$1,000.00	10%	$1,397,690.23	$1,601,099.98	$203,409.75
$1,000.00	$1,000.00	12%	$2,977,022.63	**$3,678,993.66**	**$701,971.03**

In the last example, you can see the same investment with the interest credited monthly versus annually is worth a whopping $701,971.03 more simply by choosing to have the interest amount credited to the investment on a monthly basis.

As they say, the devil is in the details, and when you are investing for the long term and relying on the compounding effects, you absolutely need to make sure you leverage your investment in every possible way.

PATIENCE & DISCIPLINE

S o by now, you should be wondering why more people are not using compound interest and time to become financially free. The answer is simple, it requires a lot of patience and discipline, and that is something that most investors don't have.

I quite simply cannot emphasize this enough; attitude is everything in doing nothing and getting rich. We have been trained early in our lives to think that overnight success is the real success, and that's absolute bullshit.

This ideology we have around success is completely flawed. The real secret to investment riches is to be patient with your strategy over a long time frame.

The power to compound interest allows anyone to become financially free given sufficient time, but there are a few things that can give you the edge:

- Invest every bit of disposable income you have
- Invest at a reasonably good interest rate (i.e. well above the rate of inflation)
- Start as soon as possible to put time on your side
- Target investments that do not require you to pay

ridiculous fees and commissions that ultimately only reduce your returns (retirement annuities are a classic example of this).

A twenty-year-old starting out investing just $100 per month at a return of 15% should, by the time they retire at age 60, have accumulated a sum just over $3,100,000. ($3.1 Million)

Can you cultivate the right attitude and be patient? If you can, you will be rich!

Don't put it off, the key to compounding is time. If you wait until you're 30 to start doing this, you'll only have around $700,000 by age 60 instead of $3,100,000.

And if you are 40 or 50 and you're reading this, don't be discouraged, time is not on your side but you likely have options at your disposal that someone in their early 20's won't.

My advice to someone in their 40's or 50's is to downscale their lifestyle dramatically for a few years and free up a major portion of their income to invest. You may not have time on your hands, but you can leverage income.

Here are some tips to get you started:

- Sell your home, start renting, or buy something

smaller. Use the additional equity from the sale of your home to start your investment, as well as putting the money saved monthly on your home to the same investment.

- Cut back on eating out, entertainment, travel, and commit to a 10 year period of buckling down to make sure you have an adequate retirement fund.

- Drive a smaller more cost-effective car, and put the additional savings into your investment every month.

You are obviously not going to be able to derive the same benefit from compounding compared to a 20-year-old, but if your start now and you leverage whatever capital you can get your hands on to start your investment and add as much as you can to it every month you might just surprise yourself and catch up.

The bottom line is don't put this off for another day unless you want to remain in the 99% and find yourself heading into retirement dependant on the charity of the system and the people around you. If you don't take action today, that's exactly what your future looks like.

MOTIVATION FROM PROFESSIONAL INVESTORS

"My wealth has come from a combination of living in America, some lucky genes, and compound interest." ~ **Warren Buffett**

"Most great fortunes are built slowly. They are based on the principle of compound interest" ~ **Brian Tracy**

"The effects of compounding even moderate returns over many years are compelling, if not downright mind boggling" ~ **Seth Klarman**

"It should be everyone's right in a capitalist system to have some way to take advantage of compound interest." ~ **Katy Lederer**

BUILDING A FAMILY DYNASTY

I always chuckle to myself when I hear certain population groups talking about being "less privileged" than others, or certain people complain about never having equal opportunity.

Listen up snowflake, the Jews as an example were heavily persecuted. Heck, they were sent to the gas chambers just for being Jewish, yet they rose above their situation and became arguably one of the wealthiest minority subsets in the world.

Yes, some people have been dealt some pretty shitty cards, the question is what are you doing about it to change the course of your family history? What are you going to do to create a new legacy for your family?

Lucky for you, I am going to tell you exactly how to get started:

- Stop spending your money on crap (start investing every free cent you have).
- Start teaching your kids about money.
- Start investing for your kids (as little or as much

as you can).

- Actively teach your kids how to invest.
- Never ever give your kids money, make them earn it.
- Take out massive life policies and leave these to your kids in a trust
- Educate your kids on compound interest

Lastly, and this is the most important thing, if you have done your job right and your kids are not total fuckups when it comes to money, make sure they continue the family legacy building the family trust, never touching the capital and always adding to the compound interest that they, in turn, will hand down to the next generation.

This is how you build your legacy and your family dynasty.

BEST PLACES TO INVEST LONG TERM

I will not be covering specific investments or investment strategies within this book as it is beyond the scope of this content. I will, however, be providing a few key points to get you started on your investment journey.

Preservation of Capital

The value of compound interest is only truly felt if you preserve your capital. This means that you must go into every investment extremely risk-averse, and seek out investments that provide some form of guarantee over your capital.

Returns VS Risk

It is worth reminding yourself that the effects of compound interest are multiplied over time and that taking unnecessary risks for a few extra percentage points would be foolish over the long term.

Diversity

Key to any investment logic is to make sure you have

a diversified approach. In other words don't put all your eggs in one basket, but equally, so don't spread yourself too thin.

Investment Ideas To Get You Started

Fixed-term deposits, money market accounts, mutual funds, retail bonds, etc.

CLOSING THOUGHTS

W hen I speak to financial advisors and investment brokers I am convinced a large part of the investment industry has lost sight of what the goal of investing really is.

If you ask most people what they are trying to achieve when they start investing, the answer is likely to be something along the lines of... "grow my money."

The average individual investors out there are not trying to beat some index or to deliver attractive risk-adjusted returns. Most people just want to make some money and build a nest egg for when they retire, which means they need to protect and grow their capital at a decent rate above inflation.

To achieve this objective, investors must understand the concepts that will help them reach their goals and stop relying purely on the advice of "so-called professionals".

It is crucial that you spend the time learning the key concepts of investing and compound interest. Once you understand the sheer power of compounding and the impact a few extra percentage points can have over a lifetime, you will change your focus and ultimately your investment strategies.

The key enemy to compounding and investing as a whole is the loss of capital. That's why ahead of earning compound interest, the preservation of capital is the most important aspect of investing. Knowing this will put an immediate end to seeking unrealistic returns on your capital, and will ensure you seek safe investments for the long term.

Understanding compounding shows why the notion of doubling your money every year, for example, is absurd. Unless you are willing to risk everything and in the process possibly lose everything!

If there is one thing you take away from this course, let it be this: Capital X Interest X Time = **Wealth**

~ ACKNOWLEDGEMENTS ~

I would like to thank my business partners, Dale Maxwell, Laura Palmeri, David Bester and Chris du Toit who have held down the fort while I took the time to write this book. Without their support and input, this book would never have become a reality.

I would especially like to thank Laura for her critical eye and constant proofreading, which helps a dyslexic, barely literate guy like myself seem capable of writing something worth reading.

I would also like to extend an extra-special thank you to my wife Andrea who as always offers constant constructive criticism and input, and unwavering support. Thank you for always making sure I have no distractions when I write and for your total commitment. I could not have asked for a better partner.

Last but not least, I would like to give an extra heartfelt thank you to David for sharing my vision and helping bring these ideas to life. Your work ethic and dedication to Global Money Academy is inspiring.

First printing, 2019.

Team 6 Investment Holdings Ltd.
5th Floor, Ritter House,
Wickhams Clay II,
Road Town, Tortola
British Virgin Islands

www.globalmoneyacademy.com

www.ingramcontent.com/pod-product-compliance
Lightning Source LLC
Chambersburg PA
CBHW072239230526
45466CB00025B/2153